7.45

ALCOHOL AND YOU

ALCOHOL AND YOU

BY JANE CLAYPOOL

FRANKLIN WATTS
New York/London/Toronto/Sydney/1981
AN IMPACT BOOK

Chart on page 36 courtesy of
Alcohol Countermeasures Program.

Drawings by Vantage Art

Library of Congress Cataloging in Publication Data

Claypool, Jane.
Alcohol and you.

(An Impact book)
Bibliography: p.
Includes index.
SUMMARY: Discusses teenage drinking,
its causes and effects, and how one
can get help to overcome the habit.
1.   Youth—United States—
Alcohol use—Juvenile literature.
[1.   Alcoholism]   I.   Title.
HV5135.C55   362.2'92'088055   80-25660
ISBN 0-531-04259-6

FOR TWO WONDERFUL
YOUNG PEOPLE,
SUE CRAIN AND
MARION HOCH

CONTENTS

ALCOHOL AND YOU

1
THE TEENAGE DRINKING EPIDEMIC

Is there a teenage drinking epidemic? Newspapers and magazines certainly make it seem that there is a galloping increase in teen drinking problems. But what exactly are the facts? Can it really be true that alcoholism and problem drinking are common among young people?

An epidemic is usually a sickness or disease that spreads rapidly. Is alcohol use and abuse spreading rapidly among teenagers?

Newspapers run headlines declaring that alcohol use by eleven-year-olds is common. Magazines insist that the number of teenage alcoholics is growing rapidly. Television features stories about young people in trouble with alcohol before finishing junior high school.

So much publicity has been given to teenage drinking that many adults assume all teenagers drink too much. Other adults insist that the media have blown it out of all proportion in order to sell copies of their publications. Opinions vary; while some people believe alcohol problems among teens are out of control, others believe that drinking patterns haven't changed a bit in thirty years.

WHAT ARE THE FACTS?

Separating facts from headlines isn't easy because words such as *alcohol* and *alcohol use* and *abuse* mean different things to different people. Many adults believe that any use of alcohol by teenagers is abuse. Some think an alcoholic is a person who lives on the streets, is malnourished, and constantly drinks wine. Other people use the word to describe anyone who is *dependent* on a drink in order to relax at night.

It is more accurate to talk about alcohol drinking behavior than to attach labels to that behavior. If we look at the studies done in the last twenty years, we see a clear pattern of earlier drinking among teens. However, it is very important to know how much they drink and where they drink before deciding that there is a teenage drinking epidemic.

Some of the facts are very clear. Between 70 and 80 percent of all teenagers studied have used alcoholic beverages by the time they are seventeen or eighteen. This has been true since 1950. But Dr. Gail Milgrim, an associate professor at Rutgers University, says, "*Use* is not the same thing as problem drinking. *Use* could mean a bit of wine with a spaghetti dinner or in connection with a religious service."

Do we really believe a teen who shares a glass of wine with the family while eating pizza is part of a teenage drinking epidemic? Can one beer at a family picnic on a Sunday afternoon label a seventeen-year-old a "teenage drinker"?

Although it's clear that teenagers and alcohol are mixing more than ever before, we need to pin down the facts before we accept the term "epidemic."

THE FIRST DRINK

We live in a society that drinks heavily, and teens are influenced by this. Most Americans use alcohol to celebrate weddings, to toast anniversaries, to welcome the New Year, to enjoy Christmas and many other special events. Although not all American families serve alcohol, most do serve it for special occasions. Headlines proclaiming that most young people have had their first drink by the seventh grade are not exaggerating. The facts confirm this, but it is important to know more than what we read in a headline. Since that first drink is usually in the home, with parents' approval, we should examine teenage drinking patterns carefully. Does a girl who drinks with her family at her sister's wedding qualify as part of a teenage drinking epidemic?

Nor is it clear that young people are taking their first drink at a younger age than their parents did. From 1951 to 1965, the average age of young people at the time of their first drink was thirteen-and-a-half. From 1966 to 1975, the average age was thirteen-and-a-third. The results of these studies were too close to show much change. What the studies do show is that for the last twenty years, most American children have had their first drink by the age of fourteen.

By the time students are in the seventh grade, 63 percent of the boys and 54 percent of the girls have at least tried alcoholic beverages. Those figures climb each year throughout junior and senior high school. By the twelfth grade, 93 percent of the young men and 87 percent of the young women have tried at least one drink.

The facts show that most young people try alcohol at least once before they are out of high school. We know that at least some *use* of alcohol is common. But can we infer from this that alcohol *abuse* is common? Not without more information.

Not all the studies agree, but it is generally believed that the number of teenagers using alcohol is not getting any greater. In 1978, the Third Special Report to the U.S. Congress on Alcohol and Health stated: "Since World War II alcohol consumption among youth increased steadily to a level of 70 percent in 1965 and hasn't changed significantly since." There does seem to be a growth in the *number* of teenagers with drinking problems, however.

Estimates of the number of young people with drinking problems ranged from 2 percent to 56 percent in recent studies. The difficulty in getting a consistent figure is due to the word *problem*.

Many adults view any use of alcohol by teenagers as a problem. They point out that every state has legal limits on the drinking age. They say that because of this alone, any teenage drinking is problem drinking.

Others believe that there is a difference between drinking in the home with parental supervision and drinking with other young people. Jewish youth and young persons of Italian descent often begin drinking at home with their parents' permission. They later seem to have fewer problems with alcohol than other groups whose religious or cultural values see alcohol as an evil.

EARLY DRINKING

Although some teenagers drink at an early age without problems, many others do have serious problems. Most experts believe that the early use of alcohol by teenagers is causing difficulties for many of them.

Loren D. Archer, Acting Associate Director for Program Operations at the National Institute on Alcohol Abuse and Alcoholism (NIAAA), said, "We're seeing a growing number of kids who are using alcohol to escape from other problems. If they start younger, they are more likely to get into drinking later in life."

It seems clear that people who have problems with alcohol when they are young will often have problems when they are older. In spite of what some think, most people do

(4)

not "outgrow" problems associated with alcohol. A recent study showed that problem drinkers in college were more likely to be problem drinkers twenty-five years later. Another study showed that twice as many high school problem drinkers as those who were not having drinking problems in high school started drinking in the seventh grade.

Although the age of the first drink has not changed much, teenagers do seem to be drinking more than they used to. And according to a poll taken by *Senior Scholastic Magazine*, even teenagers themselves believe that their alcohol use is increasing.

THERE *IS* A PROBLEM

Perhaps the most frightening news about teenage drinking is that so many teenagers drink to get drunk. Studies agree that young people are more likely to drink in large amounts when they do drink. In the national teenage drinking survey of 1974, 29 percent of the teenage drinkers surveyed said they usually drank five or more drinks when they drank.

Drinking to the point of intoxication is dangerous. As Dr. Patricia O'Gorman, Director, Division of Prevention, National Institute on Alcohol Abuse and Alcoholism (NIAAA), stated, "It's the kids who run into the *acute* problems connected with alcohol. While older drinkers often develop liver damage or other health problems, teens do not. Teenagers who drink to get drunk are usually in cars or in unsupervised places. They run the risk of accidents, fights, trouble with the law or other involvement with the police."

Although most teenagers drink responsibly, there are others who create a real problem for themselves and for society. The press, the government, educators, parents, and teens are alarmed about the teenage drinking epidemic.

There are also plenty of experts on record as being concerned about teenage drinking. Dr. Ernest P. Noble, former director of the National Institute of Alcohol Abuse and Alcoholism (NIAAA), reported to Congress:

We have a devastating problem with alcohol among youth in our country at this time. We feel that the problem at this stage is of epidemic proportions.

It is not alcoholism, but alcohol abuse and problem drinking that is causing such a problem for teens. It is very difficult to say exactly who is an alcoholic and who is a problem drinker, but a major difference is that the alcoholic is a person who consistently lacks control.

The problem drinker may hurt himself or herself, or someone else, while drunk. He or she may use alcohol in order to enjoy any social occasion. Usually, the problem drinker can quit drinking if he or she chooses.

Alcoholics, on the other hand, cannot control their drinking. Not all problem drinkers will develop into alcoholics, but many will after a period of time. It may take twenty years, or it may take only one.

Most teenagers have not been drinking long enough to be labeled alcoholics, but they can be identified as problem drinkers. Research findings show that the danger for teens comes from the *acute* effects of alcohol. Teens die in traffic deaths, get in trouble with the law, and drink themselves insensible. They are seldom affected by the *chronic* effects of alcoholism or severe alcohol involvement until a later age.

It's clear that more teens are drinking more alcohol. It's also clear that many of them are not drinking well. Most researchers believe that who chooses to drink what in which situation greatly influences the extent of the problem.

Although opinions vary and although emotions are high, these facts are only part of the picture. Before it can be truly understood, teenage drinking must be considered as part of the whole drinking pattern in the United States.

Problem drinking and alcoholism must be examined as part of the general disease which afflicts approximately ten million Americans. Before teen drinking can be clearly understood, we have to look at the social, emotional, family, medical, and cultural aspects of drinking.

It is easy to say that there does seem to be an epidemic of teenage drinking. It is much more difficult to look beyond that general statement and consider that epidemic in light of American society.

We must recognize that we live in a drinking society, where the use of liquor is accepted as normal by a large portion of the population. Teenage drinkers who have problems with alcohol are only a part of this population.

For teenagers *and adults*, alcohol is the most commonly abused drug. It is as easy to get, as easy to use, and as common in our society as aspirin.

2
ALCOHOL
IN OUR SOCIETY

Although two thirds of the adults in this nation drink, most of them actually disapprove of drinking. Researchers tell us that there is a tremendous difference between adult beliefs and adult actions concerning alcohol use.

Many adults delude themselves about exactly how much they drink. Other adults seem to excuse excessive drinking in loved friends or family members while condemning it in others. "Often, the difference between a drunk and a problem drinker is no more than how well the person is liked," says one alcohol counselor.

Teenagers, observing the discrepancy between stated attitudes and actual behavior in their elders, often ignore the advice that adults give them. If those adults can't see their own drinking patterns clearly, why should they be listened to? It is a fact that many teens who develop problems with alcohol come from homes where alcohol is already a problem for one or both parents. Teens seem to imitate behavior instead of following advice.

Not only is there a big difference between what people

say they believe about alcohol and how they act, but whenever expressed attitudes and actual behavior fail to match, there is usually conflict. People say one thing but do another. Although alcohol experts and others talk of changing *attitudes*, it is important to remember that attitudes are not as crucial as behavior.

The behavior of many adults includes excessive drinking. Right now, it is estimated that one in ten Americans suffers from a drinking problem.

As people learn more about alcohol use, alcohol abuse, and alcoholism, they learn that the term alcoholic is very elastic. "An alcoholic is anyone who feels that he or she has a problem with alcohol and wants to stop drinking," says one member of Alcoholics Anonymous.

Whenever drinking has a damaging effect on the person's life, there is evidence of alcoholism. Whether the drinker's work, social life, study habits, mental health, or family and personal relationships are affected, the possibility exists that the drinker may be an alcoholic. One of the best tests for alcoholism is the inability to stop drinking permanently.

Alcoholism used to be thought of as a dreadful moral problem for those people who drank too much and lived on park benches or in run-down hotels on skid row. Now we accept the fact that alcoholics are men, women, and teenagers from all walks of life. Most of the old-fashioned beliefs such as, "Ladies don't drink," just aren't true.

ADULTS AND
TEENAGE DRINKING

Not only are adults unclear about their own conflicts between behavior and belief, but they are even more confused about teenage drinking. Alcohol use by teens is part of the general picture of alcohol use in the United States. In spite of what

(10)

they say, many parents approve of, or "look away from" their children's drinking.

Since they are drinkers themselves, they see drinking as a normal activity, an inevitable part of growing up. We know that first drinks for kids usually take place in the home, with the parents' approval. Few parents encourage their children to get drunk, but many parents see nothing wrong with their children drinking occasionally.

Some parents are relieved when their teenagers drink rather than use drugs. Because alcohol is familiar, it is less frightening than marijuana or other drugs. Not all adults understand that alcohol is a drug. More than one adult, when informed of his or her child's use of alcohol at school or in public, has said, "At least it's not pot."

Alcohol use, like food patterns, seems to be conditioned early by family patterns. It is a fact that children of alcoholics are a high-risk group for alcoholism. Less clear is the prospect for children of nondrinkers. While most will follow their parents' patterns and become nondrinkers, their chance of drinking excessively is greater than average. Problem drinkers tend to come from the homes of either nondrinkers or problem drinkers.

ALCOHOL EDUCATION

In spite of the fact that many adults use alcohol and condone its use by teens, most view alcohol as potentially dangerous. There is often conflict between actions and attitudes when it comes to alcohol education. All states mandate some alcohol education for teens. Some states begin teaching about alcohol as early as the third grade.

The Federal Government is spending $17 million a year on alcoholism-prevention activities. However, our alcohol education programs are a crazy quilt of facts and opinions with no one recognized goal. While some programs attempt to instill values and actually teach about alcohol as a part of "moral education," other programs do no more than give the chemical facts about alcohol.

Alcohol education programs have traditionally taken the "worm in the bottle" approach. At one time, when alcohol education first began, it was considered educational for the teacher to drop a worm into a bottle of alcohol and let the class watch it die. When the worm was dead, the teacher would say something like, "Now you can see what alcohol does to your body."

Alcohol education programs have traditionally concentrated on the dangers of alcohol. It is now believed that these programs have generally been less effective because of their moralistic approach. Students who were lectured about the evils of alcohol all too often knew that their parents, their parents' friends, and even their teachers were using alcohol without curling up and dying the way the worm did.

Our traditional alcohol education programs have been in conflict with the expressed behavior of the community. As a result of that conflict, young people are suspicious of these education programs.

School curriculums are often slow to catch up with social attitudes and knowledge. Although the majority of the American population comes from a varied ethnic background, many early educators came from nondrinking, puritanical backgrounds. Many school curriculums reflect that cultural bias.

Some school curriculums were instituted during the 1920s, when the use of alcohol was illegal for everyone. The Prohibition Era, lasting from 1920 to 1933, left a legacy of alcohol education laws and attitudes which are still reflected in our schools.

Along with unrealistic attitudes toward alcohol in the schools, the community has held attitudes just as unrealistic.

The community has traditionally believed that young men have a period of "sowing wild oats" before settling down. It is commonly believed that young men go through a period of experimentation and relatively strong use of alcohol before moderating those habits in adulthood. Many people believe this pattern to be normal, but research doesn't support this belief. Research tells us that early drinkers are more likely to develop drinking problems. Heavy drinkers in youth seldom switch to a pattern of light drinking in adulthood.

Modern educators who are concerned with alcohol education feel that alcohol programs must steer clear of the "worm in the bottle" approach and give students the facts about alcohol use. "When a child understands he is at risk, he is free to make an intelligent choice," Dr. O'Gorman points out. She believes that facts should be presented so students will have a basis for intelligent choices.

MEDIA INFLUENCE

It is the aim of alcohol advertisements to sell alcohol. In the late 1970s, a rash of alcohol advertising campaigns developed, directed specifically to the teenage market. "Pop Wines" were introduced as a direct attempt to capture the youth market. Sweet wines flavored with strawberry and raspberry were developed for young people accustomed to the taste of soda pop.

"Baby beer" was a product which imitated standard beer in taste, but was below the legal alcohol limit. Teenagers, permitted to buy "baby beer," could savor the taste and pretend they were older. Advertising executives denied that they were trying to encourage children to drink. But, as one consumer observed, "No one developed 'baby beer' to capture the martini-for-lunch-bunch."

Because of public protest, Anheuser-Busch decided not

to advertise "baby beer." There had been a similar outcry two years earlier over alcoholic milk shakes. Although Heublein's Malcolm Hereford's Cows came in ice cream flavors, they were actually alcoholic drinks.

Such products as alcoholic milkshakes, strawberry wine, and "baby beer" may appeal directly to teens, but the specific campaigns are not as persuasive as the general attitudes represented by the media. Television and movies reflect the prevailing attitudes of our society and, although less common, drunkenness is still treated as a joke in many comedy routines.

Even more appealing to teens is the connection between alcohol and sexual attraction. How often do we see the gorgeous heroine and the glamorous hero talking things over in a bar? How often is alcohol presented as a necessary prelude to romance?

When alcohol is not presented as either comic or romantic, it is apt to be shown as a tranquilizer. The detective has just solved an important case, undergone a grueling windup, and then claps a buddy on the back and says, "Time for a drink."

Media presentations of alcohol do influence attitudes about drinking, but the media is also a mirror of attitudes which already exist. Today in American society, people often use alcohol to celebrate, to unwind after a busy day, to loosen up at a party, to overcome shyness, or to cope with stressful situations.

There have been many attempts to control behavior by controlling attitudes that the media reflect. Right now, beer and wine are advertised on television, but whiskey and cigarettes cannot be advertised. Tobacco and liquor industries do not advertise in magazines or comic books aimed at young people. Some of the restrictions work, but no one expects young people to avoid the inevitable process of absorbing the general attitude of society toward the use of alcohol.

As American society has become more sophisticated about alcohol, television and movies have presented more sophisticated stories about people troubled by alcohol. One of the first serious attempts to treat alcoholism was the film *Lost Weekend*. That movie made hiding bottles in chandeliers and other strange places famous.

The movie starring Ray Milland which won the Academy Award for best picture in 1945 portrayed an alcoholic who would do almost anything for a bottle. It was melodramatic, but it placed the problem in the minds of the American public forever.

Other movies which have treated the problem of alcoholism seriously include *Come Back Little Sheba* in 1953 and *Days of Wine and Roses* in 1962.

In 1974, Dick Van Dyke made a television movie titled *The Morning After*. Van Dyke is one of many television and movie personalities who have publicly proclaimed the fact that they are alcoholics.

Recently, the media have begun to pay attention to teenage alcohol problems. Several television shows have dealt with the subject. *Francesca, Baby* by Joan Oppenheimer was an After-School Special that told the story of a teenage girl whose mother was an alcoholic.

Several excellent fictional books on the subject of teenage alcoholism were written during the late 1970s. A listing of fiction appears in the bibliography.

In general, society is becoming more sophisticated about alcohol use, alcohol abuse, and alcoholism, but many old-fashioned attitudes still exist. As the media begin to reflect new educational programs and new information, the people reading books, watching movies, and listening to the radio will become more informed. The Department of Health and Human Services (formerly HEW) sponsors public-interest commercials that inform the public about alcoholism. There has even been a museum show about alcoholism.

Some alcohol educators believe that the new approaches, combined with tougher laws and general attention, will cause adolescent problem drinking to decrease. Not all agree, however.

Madonna Clifford, director of an alcohol education project at the University of Maine says:

I firmly believe that this problem will persist as long as our society continues to view drinking alcohol as a convenient solution to tension, a necessary ingredient to any social gathering, an acceptable independent activity and a substitute not to be categorized as a drug. We must make a nationwide effort to change the attitudes and behavior patterns not only of teenagers, but of our entire society.

MANY ADULTS
CHOOSE NOT TO DRINK

Although the media tend to show that some people have trouble with alcohol, the fact is that most adult drinkers drink normally. By normal use we mean they drink two cocktails or less a day, and have no physical or mental dependency. However, it is important to remember that ninety-five million Americans drink, and over ten million are classified as alcoholics. Approximately 71 percent of the adult population drinks to varying degrees.

While ninety-five million people are drinking normally, many other millions are choosing not to drink at all. The reasons for choosing not to drink are varied.

Some people are afraid of alcohol because of problems they have seen in others, or because they believe they might not be able to handle it well. Recovering alcoholics accept the fact that they can never drink normally. People who have experienced alcoholism with the unpleasant consequences of out-of-control drinking often avoid the use of alcohol for the rest of their lives. At the present time, it is estimated that there are over one million recovering alcoholics in the United States. Most of them will successfully avoid alcohol for the rest of their lives.

In addition to avoiding alcohol because of the fear of ill effects, other people choose not to drink because they don't like the taste. They have sampled alcohol on one or more occasions, and have decided that it holds no attractions.

Others have no particular repugnance to the taste, but dislike the loss of control they experience when drinking. "I don't like feeling that the world is getting away from me," one young woman says. "I just have a better time at a party when I'm sure about what I'm doing."

Perhaps the greatest group of abstainers are people who fear the health implications of alcohol use. Health food advocates usually view alcohol as harmful, and abstain from drinking because of their beliefs about nutrition and health. Many athletes avoid all alcohol because even small amounts of alcohol will impair their physical performance.

Not only professional athletes, but amateur athletes who are concerned about their physical conditioning tend to avoid alcoholic beverages. Joggers, swimmers, and dancers, as well as those who engage in group sports such as basketball, will often avoid alcoholic beverages.

While some people who are in excellent condition and want to stay that way are avoiding alcohol, another group of abstainers is composed of people with specific medical problems. Persons with a history of heart disease are often advised to give up alcohol. Anyone who suffers from diabetes abstains from alcohol because his or her body can't process the sugar in alcohol properly.

A growing number of abstainers are relatives of alcoholics. Although they have never had a problem with alcohol, they understand that they are part of a high-risk group. Since at least 50 percent of all alcoholics have one or more parents who are alcoholics, there is some evidence that people may inherit an inability to assimilate alcohol normally. As one person put it, "Why take chances? With an alcoholic father and an alcoholic aunt, I'm not going to take any silly risks."

RELIGION AND DRINKING

The United States has a population with wide differences in cultural and religious attitudes. Each of the religions in existence in the United States has a specific attitude toward drinking, ranging from permissiveness to total denial.

The largest religious group in the United States is Christian, and that group is divided into the Catholic and Protestant denominations. Within the Christian denominations it is possible to find almost every possible attitude toward alcohol use, except approval of drunkenness.

The Catholic Church generally takes the position that drinking in moderation is fine for adults but that drunkenness is a sin. Catholics have many traditional uses for alcohol, and wine is used in the Mass.

Certain ethnic groups seem to have more problems with alcohol than others. Among these are American Irish Catholics. While the debate about the causes of alcoholism is not over, the problem does seem to run in families. For years, "the Curse of the Irish" has been a well-known euphemism for alcoholism.

Other ethnic groups do not seem to have as many problems with alcohol. Italian-Americans are an ethnic group with a low incidence of alcoholism.

Protestant groups have an extremely wide range of opinions on alcohol use. Certain groups, such as Baptists and other fundamentalists, see any drinking as a sin. Mormons and Christian Scientists, although not fundamentalist in belief, are also against any use of alcohol.

Other Protestant groups use alcohol freely. They recognize alcoholism as a problem, but tend to view it as a medical rather than a moral problem. In many churches, Communion is celebrated with wine. Some groups who do not believe in alcohol consumption celebrate Communion with grape juice.

Following the Christians are the Jews, the second largest religious group in the United States. Jews use wine in many of their traditional ceremonies. Children are given small amounts of wine at an early age, in connection with religious customs. Jews often use wine on traditional occasions, but are the American ethnic group with the lowest incidence of alcoholism.

The number of Americans practicing the Muslim faith is small but growing. Muslims believe in total abstinence from alcohol. Whether Sufis, Black Muslims, or followers of Islam whose ethnic background is Middle Eastern, no true believer drinks.

Hindus also abstain from alcohol. In the United States, many people who practice Transcendental or other types of meditation as well as Yoga also follow the Hindu tradition of not drinking.

Buddhists believe in moderation. They urge moderation in drink, and some Buddhists do not drink at all. Those Buddhists who practice Zen, or are involved in the discipline of meditation, abstain from alcohol.

Some young men and women who practice meditation, yoga, or eat a diet of "health" food choose not to drink because it does not fit their beliefs. Whether it is an interest in holistic health, physical fitness, or spiritual growth, these young adults see any use of alcohol as detrimental. Although their beliefs may be personal or shared with a small group, they are firm in their abstinence.

(19)

3
TEENAGE DRINKING AND PERSONAL CHOICE

Every state has a legal drinking age. The law varies from state to state, and within the last decade these laws have changed.

During the last few years, the trend has been to raise the drinking age. Seven of the states that reduced their drinking age limits to eighteen in the early 1970s have reversed themselves recently. Minnesota, New Jersey, Iowa, and Montana raised it to nineteen, Maine and Massachusetts went to twenty, and Michigan to twenty-one.

In every case, the actions were the result of dismay over increased highway fatalities attributed to teenage drinking and a conviction that alcohol use was moving down from eighteen-year-olds to their fourteen-, fifteen-, and sixteen-year-old friends.

Not all experts agree that raising the drinking age will control teenage drinking. Dr. Gail Milgrim, from Rutgers University, said: "Lowering the drinking age from 21 to 18 did not change the number of drinking teenagers. Raising the age to 19 will not change the number of drinking teenagers either. What it will do is change the places where teenagers drink."

It is interesting to note that teens and adults often have the same attitudes toward drinking. A survey taken in 1974 revealed that 62 percent of the high school youth polled ranked alcoholism as a very important issue, 67 percent of the adults rated it as very important, 71 percent of the teens ranked drunk driving as the fifth most important issue, and so did 76 percent of the adults.

At the same time, teens and adults seem to hold the same mistaken ideas about alcohol use. Sixty-five percent of the teens and 62 percent of the adults believed that black coffee would have a sobering effect. This is not true. Nor are the following misconceptions true:

It is easy to tell if a person is drunk,
even if you don't know the person.

Mixing drinks can increase
the effect of the alcohol.

A can of beer is less intoxicating
than an average drink of liquor.

A cold shower can help sober up a person.

Also, a large majority of adults and teens did not realize that a small person is likely to feel the effects of alcohol faster than a large person.

ADOLESCENCE:
A TIME OF ESTABLISHING
PERSONAL LIMITS

Just as adults have a variety of attitudes toward drinking alcohol, teens do not present a united front. The majority

LEGAL LIMITS

Worried about alcohol abuse by
teenagers, seven states have raised
their drinking ages and thirteen more
may follow.

Age: 18
Connecticut○
Florida○
Georgia
Hawaii
Louisiana
New Hampshire○
New York○
Rhode Island○
Tennessee○
Texas○
Vermont○
West Virginia○
Wisconsin○

Age: 19
Alabama
Alaska
Arizona
Idaho
Iowa ☆
Minnesota ☆
Montana ☆
Nebraska
New Jersey ☆
Wyoming

Age: 20
Delaware
Maine ☆
Massachusetts ☆

Age: 21		
Arkansas	Kentucky	Ohio □
California	Maryland □○	Oklahoma □
Colorado □	Michigan ☆	Oregon
District of	Mississippi □	Pennsylvania
Columbia □	Missouri	South Carolina □
Illinois □○	Nevada	South Dakota □
Indiana	New Mexico	Utah
Kansas □	North Carolina □	Virginia □○
	North Dakota	Washington

□ Lower age for wine or beer
☆ States that have raised drinking .
  age since 1976
○ States considering a higher
  drinking age

of them will sample alcohol, but many will not. Of those who sample alcohol, only a small percentage will become frequent users.

Adolescence is a time for experimentation and discovery. It is also an age for taking risks. While "sowing wild oats" is probably not a necessary part of growing up, experimentation to find personal identity is certainly normal during the teen years.

"When they are aware of the facts, most teens are able to make intelligent decisions," believes Dr. O'Gorman. "Our job as educators is to make sure they get the facts."

O'Gorman and other people involved in alcohol education are particularly concerned that teenagers understand the risks involved in drinking to the point of intoxication. She also believes many teens are really not informed about what it takes to drink moderately.

Recent research indicates that parental attitudes and behavior are only one consideration in teens' decisions to drink or not. Most teenagers will follow their family's drinking patterns as adults, but parents' opinions and pressure are not as important as many think. Nor is peer pressure the great impetus toward drinking that the media insist it is.

Most teens choose to drink as an expression of adulthood, not as an expression of hostility. If we live in a drinking society, and a normal adult activity is to drink, then it can be expected that teenagers will adopt the patterns of that society. As they move toward maturity, many teens attempt to express adulthood by drinking.

We don't know as much as we'd like about the causes of problem drinking in teenagers, but we do know some things. Children of alcoholics are definitely a high-risk group. The debate is far from closed on why this is so. Some social scientists who believe that environment is the key to behavior are certain that the high incidence of alcoholism in families is a result of children learning behavioral patterns from their parents.

A great deal of evidence shows that the attitudes of parents toward drinking are among the most important factors in how youth drink. Margaret Bacon and Mary Brush Jones, authors of *Teen Age Drinking*, say:

> *Parents who drink are more likely to raise children who also drink, just as parents who abstain are more likely to raise children who also abstain. Of course, young people do not always follow their parents' example. But the drinking behavior of parents is more closely related to what their children do about their drinking than any other factor—friends' behavior, living area, religion, and so on. The connection between what parents do and what their sons and daughters do is marked.*

More and more, we are discovering through research on twins who have been separated at birth, and through studies of adopted children who live in nondrinking homes, that the case for alcoholism as an inherited disease does exist.

More clearly emotional in origin is the evidence that children who do not feel close to their parents are a high-risk group. Some evidence supports the theory that homes where both parents work outside the home may contribute to the incidence of alcoholism in teenagers.

If a teenager drinks with an attitude of hostility, if his or her primary motive is to get even with parents or others, the chances of developing a problem are increased. An attitude of "I'll show them!" is a dangerous attitude to hold according to research. Apparently, the "macho" attitude of "I'm a big man, I can hold more liquor than anybody," is also a first step toward alcohol problems.

WHAT'S IN A DRINK?

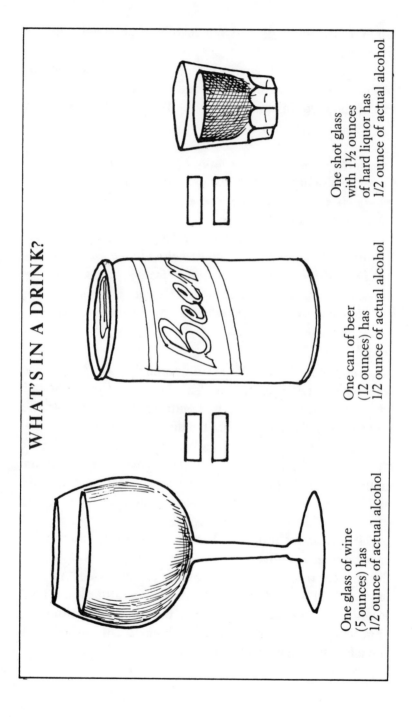

One glass of wine
(5 ounces) has
1/2 ounce of actual alcohol

One can of beer
(12 ounces) has
1/2 ounce of actual alcohol

One shot glass
with 1½ ounces
of hard liquor has
1/2 ounce of actual alcohol

Problems develop in many ways, but some of the easiest to spot are hostile attitudes or drinking to mask loneliness or feelings of rejection. Also, if you are the child of an alcoholic, there is clear evidence that you are taking a very dangerous risk when you drink.

WHAT IS SAFE DRINKING?

Anyone who chooses to drink needs to know the facts about alcohol content in drinks before he or she begins.

A "drink" of alcohol can mean anything from a straight triple scotch to a glass of beer. Knowing the alcoholic content of various drinks means knowing which drink is strong and which is weak. Sometimes the drink which appears to be weak can be surprisingly strong.

Ethyl alcohol, often shortened to ethanol, is a chemical compound that changes moods. No drink is pure ethyl alcohol. Beer, for example, is about 4½ percent alcohol per ounce. That means that (at 4½ percent) a 16-ounce can of beer contains ¾ of an ounce of alcohol. A 100-proof vodka or whiskey has ¾ of an ounce of alcohol in a 1½-ounce measure.

Wine has a higher alcohol content than beer (about 12 to 20 percent), but less than hard liquor. Whiskey, gin, vodka, bourbon, rum, and brandy are hard liquors and are nearly 50 percent ethyl alcohol. This means that a 100-proof whiskey contains 50 percent alcohol, and one shot will contain the same amount of alcohol as a can of beer or a glass of wine.

Many teens feel that they can safely drink beer. Indeed, there are adults who believe that it is impossible to be an alcoholic if one drinks only beer. The truth is that while more liquid must be consumed, beer is as intoxicating as any other alcoholic beverage.

One glass of wine, one can of beer, or one shot of hard liquor all have about the same amount of alcohol. Mixed drinks are a problem, however, because they are sometimes unpredictable. Some people will mix a drink with more than one shot glass of alcohol. As a result, that person may be drinking the equivalent of two or three standard ounces of alcohol.

The average person can burn up one mixed drink an hour if that drink contains no more than one ounce of liquor (one-half ounce of actual alcohol). If a drinker remembers that fact and considers his or her body weight, the chances are good that there will be no problems.

MODERATE DRINKING
DEPENDS ON THESE RULES

Remember that your body can probably burn up one ounce of alcohol in an hour.

Remember your weight.

Be aware of the actual amount of alcohol going into your glass.

Don't show off.

Don't drink alone.

Don't drive or ride in a car with other drinkers.

4
WHAT HAPPENS WHEN YOU DRINK

Although many drinkers speak of getting "high," and initially experience alcohol as a stimulant, alcohol is actually a depressant. One reason for confusion about the effects of alcohol is that alcohol causes the capillaries to dilate. These capillaries, carrying blood just below the surface of the skin, expand, and the skin flushes, causing a warm feeling.

When you drink, the ethyl alcohol goes directly into the bloodstream, brain, and central nervous system. No one knows exactly how alcohol intoxicates, but a great deal is known about the effects of alcohol on the body.

The alcohol is taken into the mouth and goes into the stomach where a small amount goes through the walls of the stomach and immediately into the bloodstream. Most of the alcohol goes down to the small intestine and then passes through the intestinal walls into the bloodstream.

The blood then carries the alcohol to every part of the body, including the liver, brain, and heart. It is the function of the liver to change the alcohol into water, carbon dioxide,

(29)

and energy. The process of changing alcohol to water is called oxidation.

Oxidation of alcohol in the liver takes place at the rate of about one ounce every hour. If more than one ounce of alcohol an hour is ingested, it will not be oxidized, but will keep on passing through all parts of the body, including the brain.

The bloodstream carries some alcohol to the brain almost immediately after it is ingested. More alcohol will pass through the brain until the liver has oxidized it all into carbon dioxide and energy.

Alcohol depresses brain function. It is a drug in the same class with the anestheticlike drug ether. It appears to stimulate people because it depresses those parts of the brain that control judgment and movement. A person may appear more relaxed after a drink, may become boisterous and laugh a lot. The same thing happens when a person gets ether anesthesia.

It is important to note that if alcohol is used in moderation, there do not seem to be any adverse effects. In fact, doctors sometimes prescribe the use of alcohol as a sedative for older Americans in convalescent homes.

Studies have also shown that drinkers often live longer than nondrinkers. A study done at the Kaiser Permanente Medical Care Program in Oakland, California, revealed that drinkers had fewer heart attacks than nondrinkers.

In the nineteenth century, Dr. Francis Edmund Anstie proposed a safe daily limit of 1½ ounces of actual alcohol; 1½ ounces of actual alcohol would be the equivalent of three ounces of well-diluted whiskey, a half bottle of table wine, or four glasses of beer, to be taken only at meals.

Dr. Anstie's limit as well as the more modern rule of thumb of one ounce per hour are only guidelines for drinkers. The truth of the matter is that there are so many different ways in which people react to alcohol, and so many different

(30)

factors in predicting those reactions, that no one rule is absolutely foolproof.

The NIAAA (National Institute on Alcohol Abuse and Alcoholism) report on alcohol said:

> *Drinking alcohol in moderation does the body little permanent harm. But when taken in large doses over long periods of time, alcohol can prove disastrous, reducing both the quality and length of life. Damage to the heart, brain, liver and other major organs may result.*

Although the words moderation and large doses may seem confusing, there is evidence that daily consumption of as little as four ounces of hard liquor will cause damage to some people.

Despite the many studies reported each year, there is still much evidence to come. We don't know exactly what causes intoxication, nor do we know exactly what causes alcohol dependency or alcoholism. We cannot even safely predict how quickly a person will become intoxicated, or how that person will behave when drinking.

Some of the factors which influence reactions to drinking are emotional and cultural. How a person feels when he or she takes a drink may influence the body's reaction. Three important nonchemical, nonphysical factors will influence a person's reaction to drinking: what a person expects to happen; what a person's mood is before drinking; and the setting in which a person drinks.

If a person believes that drinking is a grave moral weakness and takes a drink, he or she is inviting immediate difficulties. A person who is accustomed to seeing parents drink wine with meals may take the first glass of wine with no negative expectations. In most cases, that person will have little difficulty, unless he or she drinks to excess.

Alcohol is sometimes used as a mood changer. After the first round of drinks people will often become friendlier and more sociable at a party. It is also true that instead of changing a mood, alcohol may simply deepen it. An angry person may become angrier, and a depressed person may become more depressed.

The setting is very important when predicting the effects of alcohol. Drinking alone has long been recognized as a warning symptom of alcoholism. Drinking at a party or in social situations is usually not a problem for most people unless they drink a great deal.

Aside from these three factors, there are others which are equally important. The size of the person doing the drinking affects the rate at which alcohol is oxidized by the system. A 200 pound man can drink more alcohol safely than a 130 pound man. If they drink the same amount of alcohol in the same amount of time, the lighter person will show more effect more quickly. It has been calculated that a person's body tissues are 70 percent water. A heavier person has much more body water in which alcohol can be diluted.

Alcohol will make it difficult for a person to make judgments, to concentrate, and to understand things. An experienced drinker will understand this, while an inexperienced or neurotic drinker will refuse to recognize the fact that he or she is operating with diminished abilities.

Regular drinkers may develop a psychological tolerance to alcohol which will allow them to compensate for the impairing effects that alcohol may have. For this reason, it sometimes seems as though people can "learn to drink." What they learn is that their physical and mental abilities will be impaired, and that they must control their behavior carefully.

Psychological tolerance of this sort may fool both the drinker and his or her friends. One cannot always determine the extent of that person's ability to drive. It is important to

RESPONSES TO ALCOHOL

Removal of worry, shyness, or tension → Exhilaration → Loss of inhibitions

Emotional Depression → Quarrelsome, argumentative → Confusion, lack of coordination

Weepy or giggly → Drowsy → Loss of consciousness

know that psychological tolerance does not prevent alcohol from impairing thought and action; it merely enables the experienced drinker to cope better than the inexperienced drinker.

There is some evidence that some persons may have an "allergic" reaction to alcohol, triggered by any amount of alcohol at all. A number of recovering alcoholics claim that they were unable to operate sensibly from the moment of the first drink. These individuals often say that they experienced blackout drinking from the very beginning of their drinking experiences. As yet, there is little evidence to substantiate these experiences, but most alcohol experts are reluctant to disclaim the possibility that some individuals inherit a psychological predisposition to alcoholism, a predisposition that might be called an "allergic reaction."

THE FIRST DRINK

The minute alcohol enters the mouth, the body begins to respond to its presence. One drink does change things, but for most people one drink could not be considered physically dangerous. A person who has little experience with alcohol may find that even one drink impairs driving ability, although alcohol traffic experts have determined that it does not. Since the U.S. Department of Transportation estimates that nearly 50 percent of all fatal automobile crashes involve drunk drivers, the question of how much alcohol is too much becomes crucial.

Alcohol and traffic safety experts measure how much alcohol is in the bloodstream when discussing the alcohol content limits for drivers.

Four factors will affect the blood alcohol content (BAC) of a person: the amount of alcohol the person drinks, whether or not the person has eaten before or during the drinking, how much a person weighs, and how much time goes by between drinks.

According to traffic safety experts, an adult male who weighs 170 pounds, has not eaten before drinking, and does not wait very long before driving will be affected by two average drinks. An inexperienced drinker, or a smaller one, might be affected sooner.

HIGH, INTOXICATED, DRUNK, AND COMATOSE

If a person drinks too much, he or she will get drunk. We have seen that the question of how much is too much is an extremely difficult one to answer. Just as amount will vary from person to person, what *drunk* means will also vary.

The rich variety of words and phrases in English are an illustration of the complexity of the condition which we attempt to describe. *Tight, tiddly, high, got a buzz on, belted a few, blasted, blotto, smashed, stoned,* and *bombed* are but a few of the slang words we hear used. Legally, the word is intoxicated, but even there we speak of mildly and strongly intoxicated.

Perhaps the most commonly used word is *drunk*. What does drunk mean? To one person, the statement "I was drunk last night," will conjure visions of a person drinking himself into a blackout or comatose state. Another person might hear the sentence "I was drunk last night," and assume that it means the speaker had more than two or three drinks with dinner. The truth is that drunkenness has stages ranging from a slight impairment of physical and mental capabilities all the way to death.

Legally, an intoxicated person is a person whose mental or physical functioning is substantially impaired as a result of the use of alcohol.

(35)

NUMBER OF DRINKS IN ONE HOUR
APPROXIMATE BLOOD ALCOHOL CONTENT (BAC)

DRINKS	BODY WEIGHT IN POUNDS								
	100	120	140	160	180	200	220	240	
1	.04	.03	.03	.02	.02	.02	.02	.02	Reasonable
2	.08	.06	.05	.05	.04	.04	.03	.03	
3	.11	.09	.08	.07	.06	.06	.05	.05	
4	.15	.12	.11	.09	.08	.08	.06	.06	
5	.19	.16	.13	.12	.11	.09	.09	.08	Unsafe
6	.23	.19	.16	.14	.13	.11	.10	.09	
7	.26	.22	.19	.16	.15	.13	.12	.11	Illegal
8	.30	.25	.21	.19	.17	.15	.14	.13	
9	.34	.28	.24	.21	.19	.17	.15	.14	
10	.38	.31	.27	.23	.21	.19	.17	.16	

One drink = 1 ounce of 100 proof liquor or one 12 oz. beer

Subtract .01% for each hour of drinking

MANY TEENAGERS
DRINK TO GET DRUNK

The NIAAA says these are the facts:

*By the time they reach twelfth grade,
more than half of the young people
drink alcohol at least once a week.*

*Nearly half of all teenagers who drink
say that they have been drunk at least once—
compared to only 19 percent ten years ago.*

*Five percent admit they get drunk
once a week or more often.*

*Thirty-four percent say their
drinking habit has created problems
with school, friends, or police.*

*The average amount of alcohol
a teenage drinker consumes is equivalent
to four twelve-ounce cans of beer a week.*

*Beer is the favorite alcoholic beverage
of teenagers.*

A 1977 study by H. Blane and L. Hewitt found that 45 percent of the teenagers studied reported having been drunk at least once in their lives, and about 30 percent of the twelfth graders reported being drunk four or more times a year.

Many studies have been done and each comes up with slightly different figures, but it does seem clear that many teens are using alcohol to get drunk or "high." While there is exaggeration in the news and magazine articles, and the studies come up with conflicting figures, no one doubts that more and more teenagers are getting drunk often.

While many adults think *all* alcohol use by teenagers is a

serious problem, others point out that most teenagers who drink do not have difficulties.

Shirley Rosenberg, an editor on the "First Special Report on Alcohol Abuse and Alcoholism," wrote for *Seventeen Magazine*:

> *The latest national picture shows that at least three out of four teenagers today drink beer, wine or liquor. One third of the young people who drink get into trouble—partly because they get drunk easily, and partly because they are prone to flaunt their drinking—but there's no indication that the young are getting into more serious trouble than teenagers did a generation ago.*

Ms. Rosenberg says that there are 25 percent more teenagers in America than there were a dozen years ago; six million more young people are probably drinking today.

Dr. John Weir, director of a program to help teenagers overcome alcohol-related problems in Marin County, California, believes that most teenagers who drink handle their liquor well. Like most experts, he is concerned about the number of teenagers who drink to get drunk.

FREQUENCY AND AMOUNT

About one fourth of the older high school males and one tenth of the older high school females often drink enough to cause themselves real problems. About 5 percent of high school students are problem drinkers; that is, they are drunk once a week or more.

Statistics like the ones above are the sort that headlines are built around. Although most young people are not part of the statistics, it does indicate a real problem. Studies confirm that although young people drink less often than adults, those who do drink get drunk more frequently than adults.

In the latest national survey of teenage drinking, an estimated 24 million high school students drink. Two-thirds take small amounts of alcohol from once a week to once a month, and have no serious alcohol-related problems. Another 8 percent drink more often than once a week. Except for getting drunk often, they manage to stay out of serious trouble. But 3 percent get into a lot of trouble.

The Research Triangle Institute in Durham, North Carolina, estimates that 3 percent of American teenagers today have a serious drinking problem. Other estimates are higher. The NIAAA official estimate is that 1.3 million young men and women (about 4 percent) between the ages of 12 and 17 have serious drinking problems.

At the present time, the NIAAA estimates that there are 450,000 teenage alcoholics in the nation. Many experts believe that the early drinking patterns of teens will produce younger and younger alcoholics in the future.

Dr. Patricia O'Gorman, Director, Division of Prevention of the NIAAA, said: "Every statistic shows that kids are drinking younger. What everyone is wondering is, are we going to have more alcoholics in twenty years? We just don't know."

Dr. Don Calahan of the University of California at Berkeley says he is willing to bet that this will be the case. "The currect increase in drinking population automatically increases the proportion at risk of having drinking problems later. The reasonable hypothesis is that within the next few years we'll see a significant increase in the rate of chronic alcohol problems."

Dr. O'Gorman does not believe we have an epidemic of teenage *alcoholism*. She says, however, that the trends in adolescent drinking practices merit serious attention. "Approximately 90 percent of teenagers today have tried alcohol, as compared to an average of 53 percent in the 1950s.

In their 1977 study on adolescent drinking, Blane and Hewitt found that the 65 percent of students who had experienced getting drunk at least once were:

> *Therefore at risk for suffering acute effects of alcohol (intoxication, blackouts, gastric distress, "hangover"), behavioral concomitants of intoxication (incoordination and disinhibition, including belligerence, crying, "silliness," raucousness, impulsive behavior, poor judgment), and negative social and interpersonal consequences (fights, impaired driving, fractured relations with friends and relatives, destruction of property, job difficulties, arrests or other involvement with police).*

There is a clear distinction between the *acute* effects of alcohol and *chronic* alcoholism. The adult alcoholic is apt to be a *chronic* (long-term) alcoholic who develops a physical dependency on alcohol. He or she may suffer severe mental and physical symptoms and have a tolerance for alcohol.

There are teenage alcoholics, and their numbers appear to be growing, but most teenagers who drink do not have this disease. Teenagers generally do not have a physical dependence on alcohol, but are more apt to suffer the short-term consequences of drinking. Short-term consequences can be very dangerous or even fatal, but it would be misleading to call all teenagers who drink to excess alcoholics.

ACUTE ASPECTS
OF DRINKING

The main danger from drinking is in getting drunk. The symptoms of drunkenness may be present in any combina-

(40)

tion. Some drinkers experience only one or two symptoms, but most people who drink to the point of drunkenness will experience some of each of these acute aspects.

Loss of coordination is one of the first symptoms of drunkenness. Stumbling over small objects, being unable to perform routine tasks such as pouring gravy into the gravy bowl or catching a football may be some of the first signs of drunkenness.

Slurring or loss of speech often follows loss of coordination. In comedy routines which ridicule persons who have ingested too much alcohol, one standard mannerism which the comic will mimic is speech pattern. Cartoonists often attempt to reproduce those speech patterns. "Sposh uy shell me sakly whts swhrong, officer?" ("Suppose you tell me exactly what's wrong, officer?")

Stomach problems are standard for some drinkers and exceptional for others. Some drinkers will experience a burning and nausea, and others will vomit often. The esophagus is irritated and will attempt to clear the poison out of the system by vomiting rapidly.

Hangovers, although not part of intoxication, are another acute aspect of drinking. They occur the day after the drinking, as the system attempts to rid itself of alcohol. Hangovers do not always seem to be related to the number of drinks a person has the night before. The length, severity, and number of hangovers a person gets may depend on his emotional state as much as on the amount of alcohol he drank. There are no cures for hangovers. Drinking black coffee or water won't help. Remedies such as Bloody Marys only add to the alcohol load that the system must burn off.

One symptom of drunkenness is the personality change which may accompany heavy drinking. Most drinkers recognize that alcohol will change moods, and many use alcohol to increase sociability, but not all are aware of the dangerous aspects of personality change.

(41)

Alcohol affects the upper part of the brain where self-control and other learned behavior is stored. In some people who may have emotional problems usually kept under control by the upper part of the brain, the first drink may produce either aggressive behavior or deep sadness.

Eventually, the higher amounts or concentrations of alcohol in the blood slow down brain cell activity to the point where memory, muscular coordination, and balance are impaired. At this stage, the drinker is obviously intoxicated, with glassy eyes and thick speech, faulty memory, and a rolling or staggering walk.

Many suicides, murders, and other crimes of violence are related to alcohol. Some of them are committed in blackouts.

Blackouts are periods of time during which the drinker loses all memory. Any drinker may experience blackouts if he or she drinks enough, but some problem drinkers or alcoholics experience blackouts routinely. It is difficult to convince these persons that blackouts are not normal. Blackouts are always a symptom of trouble. Memory loss and blackouts are warning signals of alcoholism.

If a drinker drinks enough, he or she will fall into a stupor and pass out. Even though the drinker passes out, there is still risk. Each year, thousands of people choke on their own vomit while in an alcoholic stupor.

Like all drugs, alcohol does a lot of damage. Professor Melvin H. Knisely at the Medical University of South Carolina proposed that even moderate drinking destroyed brain cells. Knisely's tests strongly indicate that drinking kills brain cells through oxygen starvation. Damage may begin at what some people would call "moderate" drinking levels. The person who drinks enough alcohol to reach a state of unconsciousness will develop a substantial number of tiny brain hemorrhages, and at each of these points, brain cells die from lack of oxygen. The damage is cumulative and irreversible. This occurs whether the person drinks socially or alcoholically.

(42)

Alcohol overdose is a common cause of death. Very large amounts of alcohol (such as a quart if drunk in five to thirty minutes) may occasionally cause death by anesthetizing the brain center controlling breathing. One thousand people die from alcohol overdoses every year.

Many others who supposedly die from overdoses of heroin or barbiturates have really died from the combination of alcohol and other drugs. When alcohol is combined with barbiturates, tranquilizers, or heroin, it has an increased effect. Two drugs combined don't double the dose but each drug makes the other more potent. The effect of one plus one becomes three or four or more. This synergistic effect, caused by combining alcohol with other drugs, is highly unpredictable and dangerous.

CHRONIC ASPECTS
OF DRINKING

Teenagers often risk the acute effects of alcoholism, but have seldom drunk long enough to encounter the chronic effects.

Most chronic effects of alcoholism are associated with a long period of alcohol use and overuse. Damage to the liver, heart, or other organs is perhaps the most common. Since the liver is responsible for oxidizing alcohol, continual drinking may damage it first. Most people who die from cirrhosis of the liver are heavy drinkers. Also, the stomach may be so irritated by constant use of alcohol that it may develop ulcers.

It is too early to tell, but new research indicates that some types of cancer are closely related to alcohol consumption. These include cancer of the esophagus, mouth, and larynx.

The two most famous symptoms, "wet brains" and delirium tremens, are well known to the general public. Delirium tremens, or the "D.T.'s," are the body's response to sudden deprivation of alcohol after the body had adapted to large amounts. "D.T.'s" involve shaking, often accompanied by hallucinations, confusion, convulsions, and, occasionally, death.

"Wet brain" is a slang term for persons who have drunk so much for so long that they have to be permanently institutionalized because of their lack of mental capacity.

There are about 4,000 people in the nation who suffer from Wernicke-Korsakoff syndrome, a condition combining symptoms of palsy and neuritis, and resulting from long-term, heavy drinking. This syndrome leads to confusion and an inability to learn new information or to recall events.

Some sort of treatment is always required for alcoholism if there is to be recovery. The disease is progressive—that is, the alcoholic will always get worse if he or she continues to drink and is compelled to drink. Because of the compulsive nature of the illness as well as the progressiveness, the person cannot quit drinking without help. The eventual end of alcoholism is insanity or death. Alcoholism shortens the average life span by ten or twelve years.

5
PROBLEM DRINKING AND SOCIETY

No one who looks at the facts would deny that alcohol abuse is a costly problem in our society. The United States Department of Health, Education, and Welfare (HEW) estimated in 1978 that drinking problems cost society about $43 billion a year in lost production, medical costs, and other expenses.

HEW called alcohol the most abused drug in the United States, and said that the rate of alcoholism was on the rise. The National Institute on Alcohol Abuse and Alcoholism calls alcoholism the nation's third largest health problem, after heart disease and cancer.

Thirteen thousand deaths each year result from cirrhosis of the liver, and alcohol is implicated in many other deaths.

According to the report, about half the traffic fatalities, half the homicides, and one third of the suicides are associated with alcohol misuse.

Statistics can never express the tragedy of people's lives, but they do present a clear picture. The 1978 HEW report on alcohol abuse painted a tragically explicit picture of the scope of the problem in the United States.

*An estimated 10 million adults are
either alcoholics or problem drinkers.*

*As many as 205,000 deaths a year
are related to alcohol.*

*More than 3 million—19 percent—of the
fourteen- to seventeen-year-olds in the
United States are considered problem drinkers.*

Former HEW secretary Joseph A. Califano, Jr. said of the report, "This report documents the reality that problem drinking is threatening or damaging or destroying the lives of literally tens of millions of Americans."

Califano also has said, "Excessive consumption of alcohol takes a terrible toll on the health, safety, and happiness of millions of Americans. We know beyond a reasonable doubt that the misuse of alcohol is an immense health and social problem."

In another survey done by the University of California at Los Angeles, it was found that every alcoholic costs the country's economy nearly $5,000 a year. That figure was based on direct health-care costs of $11.9 billion, loss of wages and production because of alcoholism at $20.6 billion, and $11.5 billion lost in fires, motor accidents, and violent crimes related to alcohol.

For business and industry as a whole, the figure of $4.2 billion is widely quoted as the average yearly loss due to alcoholism. Of the 6.5 million alcoholics in the U.S., about 3 million are employed. Thus, 5.3 percent of the American work force is alcoholic.

In addition to the economic burden that alcohol misuse and alcoholism places on the economy, the quality of family life suffers. Alcoholics Anonymous estimates that each alcoholic involves at least five other people in his or her illness.

The HEW report estimated that 1.5 to 2.5 million

women have problems related to alcohol. The National Council on Alcoholism, along with many professionals in the alcoholism field, believes that alcoholism occurs with equal frequency in both sexes. Membership of women in Alcoholics Anonymous has been growing rapidly during the last ten years. A new organization, Women for Sobriety, has been formed specifically to help women alcoholics deal with their special problems.

Many believe that women alcoholics are less quick to admit their illness because of the additional social stigma placed on women by society. Recent research indicates that although women may identify themselves more reluctantly, their chances of recovery are greater. In the past, most alcohol research and treatment programs focused on men, so the evidence is still not conclusive. What does seem clear is that women alcoholics are a very special part of the alcohol picture.

Although it is a fact that most women alcoholics work outside the home, it is still true that children are most often dependent on their mothers for care. Child care may suffer in the home of a man or woman alcoholic, but many women alcoholics are raising their children without a mate. For that reason, the problem of alcoholism is seen as especially dangerous for children in homes of alcoholic women.

Approximately one third of the birth defects associated with mental retardation are the result of mothers who are problem drinkers or alcoholics.

DEFINITION OF
PROBLEM DRINKERS

Both alcoholics and problem drinkers drink too much, but there are differences between the two. For instance, a problem drinker may not drink very often. If he or she gets drunk only once a month at a social gathering and then drives home from the party, he or she has a problem. This problem drinker is running a terrific risk twelve times a year.

People with enlarged livers who drink even one martini at dinner are considered problem drinkers, because they are making their health worse. Those who make problems for themselves by drinking may be considered problem drinkers.

Most problem drinkers are able to quit drinking when they want to. If they go to a meeting or a social occasion where drinking is not appropriate, they don't drink. If their doctor tells them not to drink, they can stop. Often, but not always, problem drinkers slide into alcoholism if they continue drinking long enough.

SPECIAL TEEN PROBLEMS

Perhaps one of the fastest growing and most alarming aspects of the teenage drinking epidemic is the fetal alcohol syndrome.

In recent years it has been proven that women who drink heavily while they are pregnant tend to produce infants who are born with a definite pattern of physical, mental, and behavioral abnormalities. These differences include shorter height and lighter weight than normal. This pattern of abnormality is called the fetal alcohol syndrome.

Since over 600,000 teenage girls give birth to children each year, it is especially important that they know the facts about fetal alcohol syndrome.

When a pregnant woman has a drink, the alcohol crosses the placenta to the fetus. The alcohol travels through the baby's bloodstream in the same concentration as through the mother's. If the pregnant mother becomes drunk, so does the unborn baby. However, the unborn child does not have the ability to handle alcohol as well as the mother does. An unborn baby's liver burns up alcohol at a much slower rate;

thus, the alcohol stays in the system longer. Unborn babies can't say no to that last drink.

Children with the fetal alcohol syndrome do not "catch up" even when special care has been provided after birth. Some of these babies have abnormally small heads, severe facial irregularities, joint and limb abnormalities, heart defects, and poor coordination. Many are mentally retarded and experience behavioral problems, including hyperactivity, extreme nervousness, and poor attention spans.

As yet, no one has determined the amount of alcohol that a pregnant mother can safely drink. It is believed that a woman who drinks three or more ounces of alcohol a day is clearly risking her child's health. It may be that much smaller amounts are damaging. The most responsible decision an expectant mother can make is not to drink at all. It is not known if the father plays a part in the fetal alcohol syndrome at the time of conception or not. Drinking which takes place before pregnancy apparently does not harm the baby, but there is evidence that periodic, heavy drinking when pregnant is very dangerous.

Teens also need to know that 60 percent of the traffic fatalities among youth involve alcohol. FBI statistics show that more than 17,000 young people under eighteen, including fifty-one children aged ten or younger, were arrested in 1975 for driving under the influence of alcohol. That was an increase over 1970 of about 160 percent. The National Highway Traffic Safety Administration says that one-quarter of the high school students who drink say they have been drunk three or more times when they were driving cars.

Approximately 8,000 young Americans a year are killed in drunken-driving accidents. An additional 40,000 are disfigured. Most of these accidents were caused by people their own age.

Since 1972, the number of sixteen- to eighteen-year-old drinking drivers involved in fatal accidents has tripled.

One in three high school students reports that he or she rides in cars driven by heavily drunken drivers at least once a month.

It is not only the amount of alcohol that teens drink, but the places where they drink that cause problems. Certainly, drinking in moving automobiles is dangerous. Drinking and driving is an obvious risk. Drinking in public places such as roadside rest stops or public parks can cause conflict with the police.

Another risk that teens face is the problem of mixing alcohol with other drugs. The use of alcohol with barbiturates, tranquilizers, muscle relaxants, sleeping pills, or other narcotics can be deadly. Nor should alcohol be mixed with antihistamines or most medicines. In combination with barbiturates or methadone, alcohol can produce the last stages of alcoholism within a short period of time.

The evidence on mixing alcohol and marijuana may not be as clear-cut, but many experts are worried about that also. About half the drinking teens also experiment with marijuana, and 35 percent use it regularly (once a week or more).

Certain teens face special risks because of their emotional and psychological makeups or because of their family drinking patterns. Emotional disturbance, feelings of anxiety, insecurity, or self-consciousness are often given as reasons for developing destructive drinking patterns. Teen drinkers who start to drink for psychological reasons are apt to develop problems. Experts suspect that these teens try to skip ahead into the adult role, to gain a feeling of comfort, power, and acceptance by their peers.

Pitsa-Calliope Hartocollis, a psychologist and specialist in adolescent drinking at the Menninger Clinic, in Topeka, Kansas, says, "When the drinking is done, this teenager will feel alone, isolated, insecure. Such a person needs psychotherapy and AA."

Hartocollis tells of a ten-and-a-half-year-old potential

alcoholic who started to sneak drinks while both parents were working. "The boy showed moodiness, poor work in school, and isolation from his friends. Finally, after he had been drinking for more than a year, he was brought to me."

Although there are cases of alcoholism in persons as young as nine or ten, most young people with drinking problems are more accurately labeled potential alcoholics. The signs of early alcoholism are not always easy to spot, but personality change, problems in school, and trouble with the police are considered to be three symptoms for concern.

Of all the groups of teenagers, those who have one or more alcoholic parents run the highest risk of developing problems. Half of all alcoholics have an alcoholic father or mother. Some are quick to point out that the other half do not have alcoholic parents, but it is still apparent that children of alcoholics do run higher risks of becoming alcoholics if they drink.

If you are worried about whether or not you might have a problem with your drinking, you should look closely at your drinking pattern. Do you accept invitations to places where you wouldn't normally go, only because you know that alcohol will be served? If you're getting into trouble with school officials, your parents, or the police when you drink, or if you spend time with heavy drinkers, you may have a problem. If you find yourself wanting a drink before exams, before dates or dental appointments, you may be in trouble with alcohol.

Discovering whether or not a teenager has a drinking problem is slightly different from looking at alcohol patterns among adults. Such questions as, "Do you drink every day?" may not apply to teens. Often, teenagers depend on the ease of access to alcohol for their drinking. It is believed the real reason that teens in wealthy neighborhoods have more drinking problems than not-so-wealthy teens in other neighborhoods has more to do with the availability of alcohol than with teen behavior.

If you suspect that you might have a problem, it might be useful to talk to someone in Alcoholics Anonymous or your local alcohol center. This questionnaire may help you decide.

IF YOU THINK YOU MIGHT HAVE A DRINKING PROBLEM

Answer these questions honestly. One answer of "yes" may be a warning. Three or more "yes" answers means that alcohol is a serious problem in your life.

1. Do you use alcohol to keep from being shy or to build up your self-confidence?

2. Do you miss classes or days of school because of drinking or hangovers?

3. Are people talking about your drinking at school or elsewhere?

4. Do you think you drink to escape from worries? From studies?

5. Do you ever have problems with money because of alcohol?

6. Do you ever have to take a drink before you go on a date?

7. Does it bother you if someone suggests you drink a lot?

8. Has drinking lost you friends?

9. Are your friends heavy drinkers?

10. Do you drink more than your old friends?

11. Do you usually drink until the liquor is gone?

12. Have you ever had a blackout (loss of memory)?

13. Have you ever been in trouble with the police because of drinking? Arrested? In the hospital?

14. Do you get angry when people talk about the "evils" of drinking?

15. What do you think? Do you have a problem with drinking?

During the late sixties and early seventies, most adults were concerned about teenage use of drugs. Most adults did not include alcohol as a drug because it was familiar and legal for adults. Because of the attention paid to marijuana and hard drugs, many people thought that most teenagers preferred them to alcohol. The fact appears to be that both then and now, alcohol was the preferred drug of teenagers.

Dr. Morris E. Chafetz, former director of the NIAAA, has said, "Far and away, alcohol is the drug of choice among youth. For example, only 40 percent of senior high school boys and 36 percent of senior high school girls report using marijuana—the second-rated drug."

He continues, "All of the signs and statistics over the past couple of years have pointed to the fact that the switch is on among young people—from a wide range of other drugs to alcohol."

Some people felt that the alcohol use by teenagers represented a return to their parents' values. Others thought teenagers chose alcohol because it was cheaper and easier to get. It may be that young people have always used alcohol as their first drug, but that the press's attention has shifted from marijuana to alcohol.

Perhaps most adults hoped that the use of alcohol meant other drugs were not being used by youngsters. According to many of the alcohol treatment experts, this is not the case. Alcoholics Anonymous reports that 37 percent of their members under thirty say they used drugs in addition to alcohol.

Dr. Patricia O'Gorman stated that most of the young people who are being admitted to hospitals and treatment centers are doubly addicted. "We're just beginning to get them," she says. She warns:

> *Teenagers who drink and at the same time take other drugs, such as heroin, barbiturates or methadone, can become frank alcoholics in a year's time instead of the twenty years it usually takes for alcoholism to overtake the heavy drinker. Abuse from other drugs telescopes the effect of alcohol. It could happen in the late teens.*

6
ALCOHOLISM

Unfortunately, no one really knows why many people, including more and more teenagers, develop drinking problems. There are visible patterns, but there are no clear-cut causes for alcoholism.

Research is being carried on all the time, and as more evidence is collected, it becomes clear that there are many reasons for alcoholism. Some of the problems associated with alcoholism in the past are disappearing as alcoholism becomes a recognized health problem instead of a criminal or moral problem.

More and more medical plans in industry cover treatment for alcoholism as a part of their health programs. Alcoholism is recognized as a huge medical problem. For instance, in 1977, when the state of New Jersey became the seventeenth state to make alcohol treatment eligible for hospital insurance coverage, Senator Frank J. Dodd, sponsor of the bill, claimed that of the 30,000 beds in New Jersey hospitals, 7,500 were filled with patients who were being treated for illnesses related to alcohol.

A statement accompanying the bill said, "Alcoholism is one of the greatest health problems in the United States and is one that afflicts individuals in virtually all social and economic categories and varying age groups."

DEFINITIONS
OF ALCOHOLISM

We have seen that there is much research to be done before we can clearly define terms such as alcoholic and problem drinker. Society has come to accept alcoholism as a medical problem, but there is still much discussion about what exactly an alcoholic is.

One definition from a Public Affairs pamphlet stresses the most important aspects of alcoholism:

Alcoholism is a chronic disorder in which the individual is unable, for physical or psychological reasons, or both, to refrain from frequent consumption of alcohol in quantities sufficient to produce intoxication, and ultimately, injury to health and functioning.

Here is a second definition which is widely accepted:

Alcoholism is a chronic disease, or disorder of behavior, characterized by the repeated drinking of alcoholic beverages to an extent that it exceeds customary use or ordinary compliance with the social drinking customs of the community, and which interferes with the drinker's health, interpersonal relations, or economic functioning.

Both definitions stress the basic elements of (1) chronicity;

(2) compulsive, uncontrollable drinking; (3) intoxication; and (4) interruption of normal life functions.

While the older medical definitions insisted on some physical dependence, or at least definite physical damage before the person could be classified as an alcoholic, the newer definitions tend to be more elastic.

The essential element in any definition of alcoholism seems to be the compulsion to drink. Where there is loss of choice, there is alcoholism. The person who wants to stop drinking and stay stopped, but cannot, is an alcoholic.

The word chronicity means doing something over and over again. If a person repeats this destructive pattern often enough, he is said to be an alcoholic. Intoxication, although occasionally happening to normal drinkers, is the clearest symptom of alcoholism. A normal drinker may have difficulty understanding exactly why an alcoholic repeats self-destructive behavior night after night.

The alcoholic may not always want to admit it, but the answer is usually compulsion. When a person is compelled to drink, an alcoholic is born. That person has lost the power of choice.

Marty Mann, founder of the National Council on Alcoholism writes in her book, *Primer on Alcoholism:*

> *The victims of alcoholism only rarely set out to get drunk. Usually they wish simply to enjoy a few drinks, "like other people." This, they find to their horror and dismay, does not seem possible for them; almost every time they drink they end up drunk, entirely against their will and intention. At a later state of their progressive illness, they find matters even worse, for by then they frequently determine not to drink at all, only to find themselves . . . drinking once more to drunkenness in total contradiction to their expressed will in the matter.*

There are many theories about the causes of alcoholism, but there is no proof that one single cause exists. More and more experts in the field accept the fact that there may be many causes.

Some people assume that those who are poor have greater drinking problems, but people from every social and ethnic group have drinking problems. As alcoholism becomes recognized as a disease that can be treated, it is hoped that more alcoholics will be willing to admit at an earlier stage that they have a problem.

Despite the stereotypes of movies and novels, only about 5 percent of alcoholics end up "on skid row." Most are employed. More than 70 percent live with their husbands and wives, and work in offices, schools, and factories. To outsiders, they may seem to be living normal lives. But their families know differently.

There have been several attempts to classify alcoholics into particular personality or behavioral types. Since the causes of alcoholism are so unclear, most professionals in the field of alcohol treatment prefer to talk about types of behavior rather than types of alcoholics.

Even when describing behavior of alcoholics it is important to keep in mind that each individual is very different and will act in an individual way. Real life seldom matches textbook definitions.

Generally, alcoholism is described as having three stages. Behavior may overlap, but most alcoholics progress from first stage alcoholism including blackouts, gulping drinks, and pre-party drinking to the last stage of alcoholism, which may end in death.

The first warning sign of alcoholism is often the blackout. In a blackout, the drinker isn't unconscious, but he or she won't remember what was said or done. *Blackout drinking is never normal.* Other early signs of alcoholism are sneaking drinks, hiding liquor, or making sure that there is always a large supply of liquor on hand.

In the middle stages of alcoholism, the drinker may be struggling for control of his or her problem. Typically, the drinker denies that there is a problem and tries to quit for short or long periods of time. At this stage, guilt and fear are experienced. The drinker may deny his or her problem, but he or she is apt to become more and more afraid of it. Often, a recovering alcoholic will speak of this period by saying, "I thought I was going crazy."

The last stage of alcoholism is what most laymen believe alcoholism to be. Daily drinking is a usual pattern. All control over the habit is lost, and the body may experience severe malnutrition or liver damage. At this point, the drinker is prone to accidents and fire. There are often difficulties with family and work. Vague fears may progress to hallucinations. The brain may deteriorate noticeably, and if the person suddenly withdraws from alcohol, he or she may suffer delirium tremens. One out of every four cases of "D.T.'s" ends in death.

Medical definitions of alcoholism often refer to the last stages of alcoholism, after physical damage is apparent. As we learn more about the disease, we can recognize that the patient has suffered from alcoholism long before these conditions became apparent. It is important to know the early signs so treatment can be sought in the early stages of the disease.

TEENAGE ALCOHOLICS

Since most teenagers have not been drinking long enough to sustain physical damage, they seldom fall into the medical definition of an alcoholic. Attempts have been made to redefine alcoholism to include the teenage drinker who uses alcohol often enough and self-destructively enough for it to be a serious problem.

Most experts in the field of alcohol studies are reluctant to use the word alcoholic but refer instead to "problem drinkers" or "teenage drinkers with problems." Laypersons, including the media, have most often used the term alcoholic in connection with teenagers.

But even the experts admit they are seeing more and more young people who fit the standard definitions. "The young people we're seeing in treatment centers are most often cross-addicted," says Dr. O'Gorman of the NIAAA. "Heavy use of street drugs and alcohol are combining to produce full-fledged alcoholics at an early age."

Although the number of teenagers who drink may not be rising significantly, the number of teenagers with alcohol problems is growing rapidly. The statistics coming from government agencies and private agencies all confirm the fact that teenage alcoholism is on the rise. When the definition of lack of choice is used to define an alcoholic, the group grows astronomically faster.

The number of young people (those under thirty) in Alcoholics Anonymous increased by 80 percent in three years, according to the last official membership survey. There are young peoples' groups in every large city as well as in many smaller towns and suburbs.

More and more young people are finding their way into Alcoholics Anonymous before they are twenty-one. Here is one young person's story as it appeared in *The Lion*, a magazine published by the Lion's Clubs of America. She is a twenty-year-old college sophomore in Los Angeles.

I experimented with drugs and alcohol from the time I was 13. I gradually quit the drugs and began

*to use beer and wine because my parents didn't ob-
ject to my drinking. When I was 17 the police arrested me for drunken driving but I didn't get the
message. My drinking started to cause blackouts
and when I was 18, I had D.T.'s and I still didn't
get the message. Shortly before my 19th birthday I
was home in my bedroom sick, shaking, frightened
and I realized that this was it. I had to stop drinking. A week later I was drunk. Three days after that
it happened again. Two weeks after that I got drunk
again. At that point it became brutally clear that I
needed help and I called AA. That's a little over a
year ago and I've been sober ever since. The AA
program has completely altered my life because it
showed me how to change and I no longer need what
alcohol used to do for me.*

One AA member says, "The kids often started drinking for
kicks at twelve; usually combining booze with pills and pot.
Often, they came to AA because of a deteriorated physical
condition. For some, the party is over at sixteen, for others
at twenty-six."

One of the adjustments that AA members have been
making is to formulate a consistent attitude toward other
drugs. AA takes no official position on anything except the
use of alcohol by alcoholics, but AA members have long recognized that many of their younger members have a dual
problem.

Forty-three percent of the AA members under thirty
claim they were addicted to another drug as well as to alcohol. AA staff quickly admit that the word addicted is used
nonspecifically, but there is no doubt that the combination
of other drugs and alcohol is bringing teenagers into Alcoholics Anonymous.

(61)

THE CAUSES
OF ALCOHOLISM

As of this date, no researcher has been able to isolate any specific causes of alcoholism. Much research has been done, and many researchers are convinced that they are on the right track.

Those theories most favored over the years are all still in some repute. Just as nothing has yet been proven, nothing has as of yet been disproven. Each week, some new piece of research evidence is reported in the newspapers.

Much of the recent research has been directed toward finding out what causes alcohol abuse and alcoholism in young people. A study funded by a $322,000 federal grant from the Department of Health and Human Services will study 5,250 randomly selected persons through the year 2008. In addition to thirteen-year-olds, the sample group includes test subjects aged sixteen, nineteen, twenty-two, and twenty-five.

Of the possible theories about the causes of alcoholism the four most prevalent are: the chemical and vitamin theory, the hereditary or genetic theory, the psychological theory, and the behavioral theory.

Several years ago, the possibility that alcoholics had a vitamin deficiency and could be treated by massive doses of vitamin B gained wide attention. It offered hope for easy treatment. Vitamin therapy has lost some of its credence, but most doctors still routinely prescribe vitamins for alcoholics. There does seem to be some evidence that alcoholics are people who require large amounts of vitamin B. It is a fact that the consumption of alcohol destroys the vitamin B in the system, and persons suffering from Wernicke-Korsakoff syndrome are often deficient in the B vitamin thiamine.

The case for hereditary causes of alcoholism is based

primarily on the fact that alcoholism does seem to be "catching." As cited earlier, one half of the alcoholics in the United States had one or two parents who were alcoholics.

A 1978 Swedish study of children who had alcoholic grandfathers suggested the possibility that some children have inherited some physiological characteristics, probably within the central nervous system, that makes them more liable to have problems with alcohol if they drink.

A Polish study indicates that inborn body chemistry traits tend to make people prone to alcoholism. They point to a correlation between the effects of alcohol and the level of the enzyme DBH (dopamine beta-hyroxylase).

Many scientists believe that an inborn, possibly hereditary, factor might be responsible. They believe that there might be a biochemical element present in the alcoholic's physical makeup, but not in those without a drinking problem.

These theories are supported by strong evidence of family occurrence—not only in persons who grew up with an alcoholic parent, but even in the offspring of alcoholics who had been raised by other, nonalcoholic couples and didn't know about their real parents' problems.

There has been at least one study in which relatives of alcoholics and people with no alcoholism in the family were fed doses of alcohol under controlled conditions. The blood concentration in those with alcoholic relatives rose significantly higher than in those in the control group, and stayed markedly higher for three hours. This may signal a predisposition for alcoholism.

Perhaps the most widely accepted theory of the cause of alcoholism is the psychological one. Alcoholics have been described as persons who are dependent on others and/or infantile in their attitudes toward the world. None of the recent research, however, bears this out. It is true that persons in the late stages of alcoholism have certain personality traits

(63)

in common; it is thought that they are the result of the drinking. As of yet, no one has been able to discover a personality type apt to be an alcoholic.

The behavioral theory of alcoholism maintains that individuals use alcohol to cope with certain life situations—generally stress-related—and that they gradually develop a new set of alcohol-related problems. Often, people learn to use alcohol to cope because as children they observed the adults around them using alcohol. While it is true that some alcoholics do seem to develop in this manner, it is equally true that others do not.

Many recovering alcoholics believe they were alcoholic from the moment they took that first drink, although they did not recognize the symptoms then. These are often people who noticed at the very beginning of their drinking that alcohol gave them a sense of well-being and relief. They were tense, anxious, and nervous without alcohol and quickly learned to depend on alcohol to change their moods.

WE DO KNOW SOME THINGS
ABOUT ALCOHOLISM

In spite of the mysteries yet to be solved, we do know some things about problem drinking and alcoholism. Perhaps the most important fact for persons with drinking problems and their families is that alcoholism cannot be cured. Alcoholism is a treatable disease and the progress can be arrested, but it is generally accepted that an alcoholic will never be able to drink normally.

We also know that alcoholism seems to occur in societies and families where there are other alcoholics. Exactly why some ethnic groups have a predisposition to alcoholism is not known, but it is clear that some groups are more prone to alcoholism than others.

Black youths have far fewer problems with alcohol than Indian youths. Wealthy young people seem to have greater problems than the poor, but this may be for no other reason than availability of alcohol.

At one time, it was thought that there were more male than female alcoholics. Now many researchers suspect that there has always been as great a problem among women, but women did not seek treatment as readily. Since women alcoholics often drank in the home and were often protected by their families, they were not as visible.

Membership in AA has grown since it was organized in 1934. The percentage of women has also grown steadily. In 1968, 22 percent of the members in the organization were women, and in 1977, 32 percent of the members were women.

THE FAMILY DISEASE

Alcoholism has been called a family disease because when alcoholism hits one member, the other members are affected. The problems within troubled families are often connected with alcohol.

Child abuse is often connected with alcoholism. Wife or husband beating is also an act related to alcohol. While there is no evidence that alcohol actually causes a person to physically attack his or her family members, there is clear evidence that alcohol enables the alcoholic to act on his or her hostility.

In addition to the dramatic problems of physical violence, there are many other problems which affect the family of the alcoholic. Financial insecurity, loss of a job, medical costs, excessive spending on alcohol, and generally impractical attitudes toward money are common. Many families are ashamed of their problem and, for that reason, may cut themselves off from society.

Alcoholism isolates the alcoholic and his family from other people. Social lives are ruined for children and adults even if there is no physical abuse or violence in the home.

CHILDREN OF ALCOHOLICS

Young people who have alcoholic parents are apt to feel guilt or responsibility for their parents. They are sometimes told by their alcoholic parent that they *are* responsible. Sometimes they are also blamed by the nondrinking parent in the family. Even when they are not told so, the evidence says that they feel guilty. Actually, children are never responsible for the alcoholism of a parent.

Guilt is not the only emotional problem a young person with an alcoholic parent may encounter. Roles are often confused in the family of an alcoholic. Alcoholic parents may reverse the roles and insist that the child behave as the parent. Inconsistent behavior from a drinking parent may create confusion in a child. Because the child lacks a clear-cut model of what he or she should become, the confusion can be serious.

Because of the apparent problems for other members of the alcoholic's family, various help and support systems have been developed over the years.

Of these, Alanon and Alateen are the best known. Alanon is a group specifically formed for people who have alcoholic loved ones. The membership is composed of men and women who learn to cope with their own feelings.

Alateen is a group especially designed for teenagers between the ages of thirteen and nineteen. There are branches all over the country and anyone who has an alcoholic parent or relative is eligible for membership. It costs nothing. The purpose of the groups is to help each other learn to live with the problem of alcoholism.

In addition to Alateen and Alanon, there are several treatment programs for those living with an active alcoholic. Young people might turn to their school counselors, clergy, or social workers who can direct them to family counseling agencies or other groups working specifically with the families of alcoholics.

ARE MY PARENTS REALLY ALCOHOLIC?

Before you call anyone an alcoholic, you should look at the situation carefully. Answer these questions if you think your parent or parents may have a problem.

1. Do one or both of my parents skip meals and drink instead?

2. Do one or both of my parents have alcohol on their breaths before lunch?

3. Do my parents forget what they said or did the night before?

4. Do one or the other of my parents have to drink to decide something?

5. Do either of my parents skip the cocktail mixing and gulp down the drinks?

6. On occasion, have either of my parents stayed intoxicated for several days?

7. Once they start to drink, do one or the other of my parents always continue until they're drunk?

8. Have I found bottles hidden in weird places?

(67)

9. Do either of my parents get drunk on working days?

10. Have either of my parents injured themselves or others when drinking?

If you have answered "yes" to three or more of these questions, one or both of your parents may have the symptoms of alcoholism.

7
TREATMENT AND RECOVERY PROGRAMS

The treatment of alcoholics is concerned with two different conditions: (1) the treatment of acute alcohol intoxication and accompanying illnesses, and (2) treatment of the alcoholism itself—the addiction to the alcohol.

Whenever possible, treatment for intoxication and withdrawal from alcohol will also include treatment for the addiction. Detoxification centers all over the country are treating alcoholics for the acute stages of their disease, and as they do that, urging them to go on for long-term treatment of their addiction.

Detoxification centers are usually run by hospitals and funded by the government and/or hospitalization insurance. A person suffering from an acute stage of intoxification can be admitted by himself, his family, or the police. While he or she is withdrawing from alcohol, he or she will be closely watched for such problems as convulsions and delirium tremens by trained nurses and attendants. Sometimes, tranquilizers or other medication will be given to help combat

(69)

the nervousness that often accompanies withdrawal from alcohol.

Usually, a person will stay in a detoxification center for three to twenty-one days. As a rule, he or she will be exposed to an alcohol education program including counseling and Alcoholics Anonymous meetings.

Before leaving the center, at least some attempt will be made to get the patient to go for further treatment. He or she will be given the names and phone numbers of AA members or a list of meetings, and will also be told of long-term treatment centers available in the area.

Many other people receive their first treatment for alcoholism through legal referral. Drunk driving programs now exist in most states. The thrust of those programs is to convince people not to drink while they are driving, but at the same time, there is incidental education about alcoholism.

The National Council on Alcoholism has more than 220 voluntary alcoholism councils around the United States that refer people to treatment and provide public information and educational programs and materials on alcoholism.

Often, the drunk driving program will be led by a recovering alcoholic who is a member of Alcoholics Anonymous. A driver who has been referred to the courts because of his driving record will be urged to look at his total drinking pattern.

Other legal referrals sometimes occur when a person is charged with a crime involving alcohol. It is not unusual for a defendant charged with disturbing the peace to be sentenced to a probation period which includes attendance at an alcohol counseling center or Alcoholics Anonymous.

New Jersey is probably typical in that it is estimated that 35 percent of all the criminal cases heard in its Municipal Courts are related to alcohol. The defendants were either drunk at the time of arrest or alcohol was somehow involved.

In New Jersey and many other states, a judge may offer

an opportunity for treatment and stay prosecution pending the results of the treatment. A defendant may be required to spend thirty days in an inpatient facility and then sixty days as an outpatient before the court dismisses charges. Sometimes a defendant might be required to attend a four-session seminar on alcohol abuse or to attend several AA meetings.

More and more doctors being asked to treat patients for illnesses such as hepatitis, cirrhosis, or high blood pressure are investigating the patient's drinking record. If a pattern of alcoholism appears to be developing, the doctor may refer the patient to a treatment center or an organization such as AA.

At one time psychiatrists and psychologists believed that alcoholism was a symptom of emotional disturbance. Many attempted to treat the emotional illness without arresting the drinking. In the last fifteen years, most psychologists and psychiatrists have recognized that they cannot treat alcoholism without arresting the disease. Often, they will insist that their client attend a recovery-support group such as AA while they are in treatment. Few psychiatrists or psychologists claim to be able to "cure" the alcoholic so that he or she can return to normal drinking patterns.

TREATMENT PROGRAMS

Thus far, Alcoholics Anonymous is the most effective treatment known for alcoholism. Experiments with counseling, vitamins, and behavioral modification, while promising, have not been able to claim as great a rate of success as AA.

Alcoholics Anonymous now numbers over one million recovering alcoholics who have achieved permanent sobriety. Many of them are young people.

One treatment program for alcoholics is actually located on a college campus. George Pressley, director of the Nassau

Community College program states, "The college problem, a spillover from the major public problem, does not provoke public attention, but booze abuse has resulted in poor studying, poor grades, impaired personal relationships, and misapplication of hard-to-find educational dollars."

The Nassau program is training students to assist others in dealing with alcohol abuse. According to Mr. Pressley, "Peer counselors are more effective than mature counselors in building confidence among young alcoholics."

One of the long-term services which helps to control addiction is psychotherapy counseling which will help the patient learn to trust others, to handle problems better, and to find the underlying reasons for drinking.

Sometimes group therapy helps the patient relate to other people and understand his or her alcoholism. Often, family therapy is indicated. Since alcoholism affects every member of the family, other members often need to learn to handle their reactions to a patient's alcoholism and to make family life more acceptable to everyone.

Behavior modification uses techniques of rewarding a patient for not drinking and punishing him or her for drinking. One type of medical help is similar. Some patients may choose to take a drug called antabuse. Because it produces nausea in combination with alcohol, a person who is taking antabuse seldom drinks. The results are too painful.

There are various social agencies available to alcoholics who may need special help. For example, vocational and occupational rehabilitation programs help people develop job skills or go to school.

At times, alcoholics may need emergency help for food, clothing, or shelter. There are various governmental and private agencies that provide such care.

Usually, the alcoholic will use a combination of one or more of these services during a basic recovery program. Alcoholism services are offered in many places, including special detoxification centers and community hospitals. Veteran's hospitals often specialize in alcohol care.

In addition to hospitals, there are outpatient clinics for the alcoholic who is living at home and needs counseling. There are mental health centers which offer a full range of alcohol services.

Halfway houses are shelters for alcoholics who are homeless or need the moral support of a new environment before they move out into the world again.

Most states also have residential rehabilitation centers for permanent cases, and state mental hospitals often offer long-term alcohol care.

The cost of alcohol treatment varies a great deal. It can be free or expensive, depending on the economic status of the patient and the type of plan chosen.

Some groups, like AA, depend wholly on voluntary contributions. The custom in AA is to donate anything from nothing to a dollar per meeting. No contributions are accepted from nonalcoholics.

Many nonprofit and government supported clinics charge according to the patient's ability to pay. Some have sliding scales that range from $5 to $25 per counseling session. And medical insurance now covers some alcoholism services.

Private psychiatric care or private alcohol treatment hospitals can be very costly. But it is important to remember that cost does not necessarily ensure recovery.

ALCOHOLISM
IS NOT HOPELESS

There was a time when people who were alcoholics were considered hopeless bums, fit only for the junkpile of life. Now it is realized that alcoholism is a disease, but not a hopeless one.

Alcoholics can never return to normal drinking, but the majority of them can return to a normal life. If long-term abstinence is considered a cure, then the evidence is clear that alcoholism can be cured. Over 50 percent of the alcoholics who seek treatment are able to achieve long-term sobriety.

For many recovering alcoholics, returning to normal life is all they need. For others, counseling and rehabilitation may be necessary before they are able to function fully.

FOR FURTHER INFORMATION

HELP FOR YOU
OR SOMEONE YOU KNOW

If you or someone you know wants immediate help for a drinking problem, the telephone directory is your fastest way. Look up any of these entries in the phone book and someone will give you aid. Everything will be confidential.

Alcoholics Anonymous
Alateen
Alcoholism Information
Alcoholism Services
National Council on Alcoholism
Women for Sobriety

It should not be necessary to pay for information from or the services of these organizations. Beware of unqualified and expensive practitioners who claim to have a cure for alcoholism.

In the case of a person who is medically endangered, call your doctor, the police, or the local detoxification center.

For long-range information and counsel where there is no emergency, you may still want to contact your local organizations. Or you may write to these organizations. You can be sure that everything will be confidential.

Alanon Family Group Headquarters
P.O. Box 182, Madison Square Station
New York, NY 10010

Alcohol and Drug Problems Association
1101 15th St. NW
Washington, DC 20005

Alcoholics Anonymous World Services
Box 459, Grand Central Station
New York, NY 10017

American Council on Alcohol Problems
119 Constitution Avenue NE
Washington, DC 20002

Department of Human Resources
National Institute on
Alcohol Abuse and Alcoholism
PO Box 2345
Rockville, MD 20852

National Council on Alcoholism
733 Third Avenue
New York, NY 10017

Rutgers University
Center of Alcohol Studies
New Brunswick, NJ 08903

Women For Sobriety
Box 618
Quakertown, PA 18951

FOR FURTHER READING

Any public library will contain several books on alcoholism. Often, the library will maintain a folder of pamphlets and news clippings as well. Here is a list of sources which may be especially helpful for young people.

Alcoholics Anonymous. *Alcoholics Anonymous.* New York: AA World Services, 1976. This is the "big book" of AA which describes the principles of the program and tells of alcoholics who have found recovery through AA principles.

Ayars, Albert L., and Milgram, Gail G. *The Teenager and Alcohol,* New York: Richards Rosen Press, 1970. Short and accurate. This book is recommended by the National Institute on Alcohol Abuse and Alcoholism.

Cross, Wilbur. *Kids and Booze: What You Must Know To Help Them.* New York: E. P. Dutton, 1979. Recent and inclusive study of teenagers' use of alcohol.

Haskins, James. *Teen-age Alcoholism.* New York: Hawthorn Books, 1976. Useful general information. This book gives examples of alcoholism and how and why teens drink. Clearly written in a simple style.

Milgram, Gail G. *What Is Alcohol? And Why Do People Drink?* New Brunswick, N.J.: Center of Alcohol Studies, Rutgers University, 1975. This is an authoritative 25-page pamphlet which is full of information and written clearly.

Pamphlets are available from many sources including:

> National Clearinghouse
> for Alcohol Information
> P.O. Box 2345
> Rockville, MD 20852

National Council on Alcoholism
Publications Department
733 Third Avenue
New York, NY 10017

Public Affairs Pamphlets
381 Park Avenue South
New York, NY 10016

Superintendent of Documents
U.S. Government Printing Office
Washington, DC 20402

There are several excellent fiction books about young people whose lives are affected by alcoholism. Among them are these novels, some based on true cases:

Glass, Frankcina. *Marvin & Tige*. New York: St Martin's Press, 1977. Story of an eleven-year-old black boy and his friendship with a middle-aged white alcoholic.

Miner, Jane. *No Place To Go*. New York: Scholastic, 1981. Easy-to-read novel about a teenage boy who drinks too much.

Miner, Jane. *Why Did You Leave Me?* New York: Scholastic, 1980. Teenage girl must face new adjustment when her alcoholic mother joins AA and returns home. Authentic writing about AA.

Neville, Emily Cheney. *Garden of Broken Glass*. New York: Delacorte Press, 1975. Newbery Award winning novel of a thirteen-year-old boy's attempt to deal with an alcoholic mother.

Oppenheimer, Joan. *Francesca, Baby*. New York: Scholastic, 1976. Moving story about a girl whose mother is an alcoholic. Good picture of Alateen group.

Oppenheimer, Joan. *The Lost Summer*. New York: Scholastic, 1977. Teenage girl who tries to hide behind alcohol as she faces problems of growing up.

Ryan, Elizabeth. *Life Is a Lonely Place: Five Teenage Alcoholics*. New York: Scholastic, 1980. This book combines cases studies of teenage alcoholics with information about alcoholism.

Scoppettone, Sandra. *The Late Great Me*. New York, G. P. Putnam's Sons, 1976. Story of a teenage girl's descent into alcoholism. Vivid and dramatic.

INDEX